The Great Wall of China
Trek Journal

Zanzilly Publishing

Copyright © 2020 by Zanzilly Publishing

All rights reserved. No part of this book may be reproduced without written permission of the copyright owner.

This journal belongs to

_____
_____
_____

Joining The Trek

Trek Date :

Check In Time :

Departure Time :

Flight Number :

Airline :

Airport :

Transport Arrangements :

The Outbound Flight

I sat with :

I ate :

Film(s) I watched :

Reading material :

Doodle Page

Flight Memories

The First Night

Accommodation Name :

Our First Meal :

I'm Sharing With :

Our Tour Guide Is :

First Impressions

Hopes and Fears

Day One

From-To :

Distance :

Weather :

I Walked With :

New Words :

Notes :

Doodle Page

Day Two

From-To :

Distance :

Weather :

I Walked With :

New Words :

Notes :

Doodle Page

Day Three

From-To :

Distance :

Weather :

I Walked With :

New Words :

Notes :

Doodle Page

Day Four

From-To :

Distance :

Weather :

I Walked With :

New Words :

Notes :

Doodle Page

Day Five

From-To :

Distance :

Weather :

I Walked With :

New Words :

Notes :

Doodle Page

Day Six

From-To :

Distance :

Weather :

I Walked With :

New Words :

Notes :

Doodle Page

Day Seven

From-To :

Distance :

Weather :

I Walked With :

New Words :

Notes :

Doodle Page

Day Eight

From-To :

Distance :

Weather :

I Walked With :

New Words :

Notes :

Doodle Page

Day Nine

From-To :

Distance :

Weather :

I Walked With :

New Words :

Notes :

Doodle Page

Day Ten

From-To :

Distance :

Weather :

I Walked With :

New Words :

Notes :

Doodle Page

We Did It!

Use this space for the triumphant group photo

And Now To See The Sights

My Favourite Memory

Best Food Experience

Worst Food Experience

How Do You Feel The Trek Has Changed You As A Person?

Can I Have Your Autograph Please!

Notes and greetings from your fellow trekkers

Going Home

Date :

Check In Time :

Departure Time :

Flight Number :

Airline :

Airport :

Transport Arrangements :

Check out our other titles at:
http://bit.ly/ZanzillyAmazon

Printed in Great Britain
by Amazon